TABLE OF CONTENTS

INTRODUCTION

I want to thank you for choosing this book, '*Lifestyle Mastery Emotional Intelligence - Master Your EQ (Self-Awareness, Self-Management, Social Awareness, and Relationship Management).*'

Communication is one of the most important parts of our lives. I am sure that most of us must have realized this along the way and, if you haven't, then it is time that you did! Take a moment to think about it and gain some perspective. Think about your usual day and how you spend it, and soon you will realize that communication plays a major role in your life. Whether you are aware of it or not, you are constantly communicating with others. At times this communication is verbal and at times non-verbal. At times it is deliberate and at times it is purely instinctive. Regardless of the form it takes, it is still considered to be communication. How does this relate to emotional intelligence?

Learning to communicate effectively and efficiently is necessary for being successful in life. This is one of the most important interpersonal skills. Tactlessness, inability to control emotions and introversion are some of the reasons why a lot of people struggle with communicating effectively. Most of these reasons can be easily fixed or reduced by learning to control your emotions and working on your emotional intelligence. When you let your emotions get in the way of how you react to a situation, you tend to limit yourself. You not only limit your responses, but you also limit other's perceptions of you.

In this book, you will learn about emotional intelligence, the benefits it offers, the principles that guide emotional intelligence and the different facets of emotional intelligence. The four facets of emotional intelligence are self-awareness, self-management, social awareness and relationship management. You will not only learn about these four concepts but also read certain tips and steps you can follow to inculcate these necessary skills. These skills will come in handy in all aspects of your life- professional as well as personal!

So, if you are ready to learn more about this wonderful concept, then let us start without further ado!

CHAPTER ONE: ABOUT EMOTIONAL INTELLIGENCE

You might have probably heard the phrase "emotional intelligence" on the Internet or elsewhere. It is a buzzword these days and there are several studies that are being conducted in this field. This phrase is thrown around in conversations quite often, but not many understand this concept. So, if you are curious to learn more, then read on.

WHAT IS EMOTIONAL INTELLIGENCE?

Emotional intelligence essentially refers the way an individual evaluates, perceives and controls their emotions. We all tend to experience and display a wide gamut of emotions like anger, happiness, irritation, sadness, boredom and such. Emotions can be positive as well as negative. Most of us tend to flit from one emotion to another one within a couple of seconds as the circumstances change. Imagine a situation where you can react in a calm and cool manner regardless of the circumstances? Emotions, when left uncontrolled, can easily drain away your energy and positivity. However, once you learn to control your emotions, you will be able to process things calmly and have a chance to react in a logical manner without letting emotions overshadow your decisions.

It is quintessential that you learn to keep your emotions in check and keep them balanced. You certainly cannot stay perpetually angry with someone you had a recent quarrel with, and you cannot be upset about something that happened over the previous weekend. Similarly, it isn't always possible to be happy and there must be some place for sadness too. It does teach you a lot and you don't have to think of things negatively if you let it go. The problem is that a lot of people tend to knowingly or unknowingly hold onto these negative thoughts, and they tend to fester more negativity in the long run. The result of this is a negatively charged environment and thinking process that adversely affects every good thing that comes your way.

So, you must learn to be in control of your emotions and must know which emotion to display in a given circumstance. Once you get a hang of it, it means that you possess a high level of emotional intelligence and vice versa. Some people are naturally good at this and others need to struggle to even realize this. All this is fine and emotional intelligence is something that you can work on provided you are aware of it. If you tend to feel that your emotions weigh you down, then understand that your emotions are ruling your life instead of you being in control. This might happen if someone has a low self-esteem or when someone is used to continual disappointments. However, until you assume control of your emotions and take responsibility for them, you will never truly be in control. You must try to understand why you feel the way you do, gain some perspective and accept the various aspects of an emotional response so that you can function logically. For instance, if someone you love dies, then being sad and crying is quite acceptable and even expected. However, if you let that grief control your life to the extent that you aren't able to function normally, then that's not desirable. Please understand that you must control your emotions and it must never be the other way around.

So, when did this concept come about? The concept of emotional intelligence is relatively new. Yes, humans have been exhibiting and feeling emotions since time immemorial, but only recently did people start researching about this topic. In 1983, Howard Gardener realized that the regular IQ tests weren't fully adequate in terms of measuring an individual's intelligence. He understood that there was more to measuring a person's intellect than mere logic. That's when he came up with a theory to understand an individual's true intelligence and for that one must consider emotional responses along with the logical ones.

In 1985, Wayne Payne came up with the term "Emotional Intelligence" in his book "A Study of Emotion: Developing Emotional Intelligence." This term gained popularity and is part of common parlance these days. Most of us refer to it as EI or EQ (emotional quotient- just like intelligence quotient). A higher level of EI means that an individual is better at communicating with others and it increases the chances of success too. This success isn't restricted to professional success alone and it refers to success in social and personal lives too.

Therefore, if you can control your emotions, then you will always be better equipped while dealing with any situations when compared to someone who cannot control their emotions or come to terms with them.

WHAT IS THE PURPOSE OF THIS CONCEPT?

As is obvious from its name, it is related to an individual's emotions. The purpose of EI is to understand how capable an individual is in terms of the ability to identify, control, evaluate and display his or her emotions. There is only such much that logic can do for you unless you have a good level of emotional intelligence. If a person is devoid of emotional intelligence, then such a person cannot make the most of their potential in life. Someone with a high level of emotional intelligence will be able to build lasting relationships, display empathy and effectively communicate with others while making them feel comfortable. Low emotional intelligence suggests that an individual doesn't feel like he or she is in control of their emotions and often blames everyone else and the circumstances for their reactions instead of evaluating their behavior.

Emotional intelligence holds a different value to every individual and the way in which you choose to develop it depends solely upon your needs and desires. For instance, those who deal with child abuse in a professional capacity are quite aware of the fact that they cannot get emotional about their work and must not react emotionally to the cases presented before them. Being emotional in such situations will do the said person no good and can prove to be quite a challenge when they have to dispense their duties. If you want to stay professional in something that has an effect on your emotions, then you must be able to keep those emotions in check. For instance, how do you think all those who work in a hospice maintain their cool? They are always surrounded by individuals who are at the end of their lives and their job is quite important. Now, think of someone with a low level of emotional intelligence in such situation and his reaction to the stimulus related to death will often be negative and it can take a toll on his mental/emotional wellbeing. Emotional intelligence allows you to detach yourself from all such negativity and instead rationalize a situation while reigning in your emotions.

CHAPTER TWO: PRINCIPLES OF EMOTIONAL INTELLIGENCE

In this section, you will learn about the different principles of emotional intelligence so that you can start using them in your life.

PERCEPTION

Perception is the ability to understand the emotions of others. It is one of the most important aspects of emotional intelligence since it helps you formulate an apt response according to the situation. It is akin to a trigger. Usually, we all tend to perceive emotions rather automatically. However, for some people, this response isn't easy and requires some effort. There are different ways in which you can perceive emotions- like sound, sight, touch, expression, tone, words, body language and such. It is time that you take a look around you and try to figure out whether the people in your life are happy or sad by merely observing them. Why is this so important? Signs and signals are present in plain sight, but not many understand them. For instance, broaching the subject of your promotion when your manager clearly looks upset about something is not a good idea.

Once you start to learn to perceive what others feel, then it helps unlock new avenues and even enables you to better understand a situation. Only when you perceive what others feel will you be able to be empathetic toward them.

REASON

Once you work on perception, the next step is to reason with that perception to formulate your emotions. Someone with a low level of emotional intelligence might think that the reasonable response to anger is anger, but that's not what a person with high emotional intelligence will do. Instead, such a person will try to stay calm even in a trying situation. This is possible because of the internal reasoning that takes place in their brain that enables them to use their emotions in a better way.

This certainly makes emotional intelligence a great attribute for anyone who works in a field of listening to troubled people. A teacher with emotional intelligence will be able to reason with a child who is acting in an inappropriate manner instead of getting angry or irritated. A counselor will be able to show empathy towards their client instead of feeling frustrating while listening to a person repeat their troubling story multiple times. Emotional intelligence helps you understand why someone is behaving the way they do, instead of allowing any negative emotions get in the way of a logical response.

UNDERSTAND

Being able to perceive an individual's emotions is the first step. After this, you need to understand why the person is exhibiting such emotions. There can be a variety of reasons and you need to understand all these reasons before you jump to any conclusions. This certainly will not come easy. It takes some time before you can fully implement this practice. For instance, a parent with emotional intelligence will try to understand why their child is behaving the way he is instead of immediately getting mad at them. Emotional intelligence, response and understanding are all helpful attributes that contribute to empathy. You might think that feeling empathy means that you feel sorry for someone. Well, that's wrong. Being empathetic means that you can place yourself in someone else's shoes and the ability to understand what it feels like in a specific situation.

MANAGE

Emotional intelligence essentially boils down to managing your emotions. If you don't think you have any control over your emotions or that you cannot manage them, then it is time that you try to rectify this. In life, there will always be times when you must speak up and times when you need to stay calm. Every circumstance demands a different approach. You cannot react to every situation without thinking about it and managing your emotions. Whenever you are dealing with any situation, you must ensure that your thoughts and emotions are in sync and undertake the appropriate action according. If that doesn't happen, then there will be miscommunication and it can result in you hurting someone or being hurt yourself. In any situation in life, you must try to analyze and think logically about the situation before you react. This helps you manage your emotions. You will learn more about all this in the coming chapters.

CHAPTER THREE: WHY IS EMOTIONAL INTELLIGENCE IMPORTANT?

Emotional intelligence is one of the most widely researched areas these days. People are extremely curious about how this affects them in their lives. Emotional intelligence is not just important is professional life, but personal life too. Before you start learning about the necessary skills to develop emotional intelligence, you must understand the different benefits it offers.

MENTAL WELL-BEING

Being aware of your emotions certainly helps you deal better with a lot of emotional problems. It will impact your outlook and attitude in life and helps reduce anxiety while controlling any mood swings. Once you are in control of your emotions and you can deal with them effectively, it helps reduce the likelihood of experiencing any issues related to your mental health. You might have come across people who seem to do well and keep calm even in stressful situations. It doesn't mean that they were born with any special skills. It all boils down to being in control of your emotions and dealing with them in an appropriate manner. When you let your emotions guide you, you will end up in sticky situations that are easily avoidable. When you stay calm even under a stressful situation, you can come out unscathed.

RELATIONSHIPS

When you can control and manage your relationships, then you will be able to effectively communicate what you intend to in a well-thought-out manner. It helps you understand others and their feelings. All this helps strengthen relationships. You can have a genuine and healthy relationship with someone only when you understand them, their emotions and their responses! A person with a good level of emotional intelligence will not let their emotions stop them from progressing in life. Also, it makes them great listeners!

PHYSICAL WELL-BEING

Stress is unhealthy and it has several physiological manifest-ations. This is one thing that can affect your overall wellbeing and is closely related to emotional intelligence. We all live in an incredibly stressful world with stressors all around us. To manage stress, you must be aware of your emotional state and control your emotions. This is incredibly important to maintain good health. Emotional intelligence helps control stress and therefore, it helps control several stress-induced disorders like hypertension and helps your body get rid of any stress-inducing hormones. When you shut down emotionally and stress overtakes you, your body shifts into the flight or fight mode and this is not desirable. The human body is incapable of identifying a natural stressor (like famine or anything that's life-threatening) and an emotional stressor (like an argument with your loved one) and tends to have a same physical reaction in both the situations. This response hinders your body from functioning optimally and emotional intelligence helps fix this. Learning to manage and control stress is an invaluable skill these days.

RESOLVING CONFLICTS

It certainly becomes quite easy to resolve or avoid conflicts when you try to understand them, perceive their emotions and empathize with them. When you can understand what others need, it automatically makes you better at negotiations. Take a moment and think about it, when you know what others need, isn't it easier to give them what they want for something that you want?

For instance, a manager with emotional intelligence will not just merely consider what he wants but will also be aware of the fact that his team members will work better if there is an incentive in it for them. By taking all of this into consideration, it certainly becomes easier to introduce a new idea while guaranteeing a favorable response from the team.

SUCCESS

The way you deal with your setbacks and your mistakes says a lot about the kind of individual that you are. A person who is emotionally intelligent understands that setbacks are just a part of the life and no matter what it is always important to just keep going. Instead of viewing a setback as a failure it is better if you can do something to get yourself back on track. You need to pick yourself up and keep going. This is part of life and you will have to be mindful of how far you would let your setbacks affect you. You will need to keep your negative emotions in check, and you must not let them go out of control, doing this will make you more resilient. A person with emotional intelligence knows that hurdles are a part of the route to success. Also, if you can effectively communicate with others what you expect of them and understand what you need to do to attain your goals, it does get easier to become successful in life.

LEADERSHIP

All good leaders tend to have one thing in common and that is their high degree of emotional intelligence that is combined with the much more traditional requirements like talent, work ethics, ambition, drive and so on. More than cognitive ability, emotional intelligence tends to differentiate those who are in senior leadership roles from those who are just above average. The higher the rank a person holds in any organization, the higher their emotional intelligence will be. When you understand others only then will you be able to deal with them in a positive manner that encourages them to do better. No one likes a leader who pushes his opinions on others. Instead, everyone likes a leader who is willing to listen, able to explain things and who is empathetic. All these skills are byproducts of emotional intelligence.

CHAPTER FOUR: ABOUT SELF-AWARENESS

Self-awareness is quintessential for personal growth. The benefits translate into better understanding of yourself as well as the way you interact with others. There are a lot of misconceptions about self-awareness. Some people seem to think that being self-aware translates into being conceited or full of themselves and don't have any space in their life to think about others. Being around a self-obsessed person certainly isn't fun! However, this isn't what self-awareness means.

Self-awareness is the ability to see things clearly from different perspectives without any bias or judgment. Once you are self-aware, then you will be able to observe your feelings, the way you feel and even notice your reactions to certain things that have a direct impact on your and everything around you. Once you are self-aware then you can reduce the chances of being completely thrown off by things that happen around you, any inappropriate moves that you might make while responding to these happenings and you will be able to reduce the chances of repeating the same mistake over and over. Your essence as an individual stays the same, you just become more aware of yourself and this helps you to stay in control.

When you are fully aware of yourself, you will be able to trust your instincts. You can learn from the past and learn to separate an emotion from instinct. All this enables you to react logically instead of emotionally. For instance, if you are writing a story, then you will want to know everything about the main character in the story- no detail is too small, and nothing must stay unnoticed. You are the protagonist in your life, and it is obviously in your best interest to learn to be conscious of the things that you do and the reasons for why you do them. You are way more interesting than any fictional character will ever be. When you are truly aware of yourself, then you will be equipped to deal effectively and efficiently with all the challenges that come your way without indulging in any self-destructive behavior.

BENEFITS

In this section, you will learn about the different things that you stand to gain by being self-aware.

UNDERSTAND YOURSELF

Your knowledge of yourself will guide all the decisions you make in life. If you are aware of the fact that you cannot function optimally with a couple of hours of sleep, then you will be able to take the necessary steps to fix this issue. You can try different remedies to get better sleep or even adjust your schedule to get the rest you know that your body needs.

PROACTIVE

Most of us are reactive in life and not proactive. We all tend to react to the things that happen around us and this often tempts us to victimize ourselves. However, when you start being proactive, you will be better equipped to deal with things and can actively take those steps to advance in life.

LEARN YOUR WORTH

We all tend to take things personally- either consciously or unconsciously. No one else has to tell you about your strengths, flaws, talents or weaknesses. If you take a moment to think about it, you are already aware of all these things. If someone is incapable of seeing your true worth, then that's his problem and not yours. You don't have to waste your time or energy trying to prove to someone else that you are a worthy human being. You don't have to expend any energy to change someone else's opinion about you. Once you realize your worth, you can start focusing on things that do matter to you. You must accept a simple truth in life- regardless of what you do or how hard you try, you cannot please everyone and make peace with this fact.

MISTAKES LEAD TO GROWTH

You will not think of a failure as the end of the world and will instead think of it as a chance to do better. You will stop beating yourself up about the mistake that you make and will think of it as a lesson to learn. In life, seldom will you be able to get something right on the first attempt. With self-awareness you will finally be able to accept this truth.

THE REASON

Once you are self-aware, your behavior will not shock you. It doesn't mean that you will not be surprised when you do something that you earlier thought was impossible. It simply means that you are aware of the reasons for your behavior.

BETTER RELATIONSHIPS

Once you start being honest about yourself, then you will be able to understand what your loved ones are trying to convey even if the words that they used are critical or when you are being given any unsolicited advice. Maintaining a façade is truly exhausting. If you never let others see who you really are, you cannot have any genuine relationships in life. A person who is self-aware will not try to hide their true persona. When you are aware of who you are and are being honest about it, you will be able to cultivate open, honest and genuine relationships in life.

PURSUE YOUR GOALS

When you know who you are as a person, then you will be aware of what you want in life. Once you have certain goals in mind, self-awareness enables you to take all the necessary steps to achieve your goals. For instance, if you are to attain something and when you are aware of your pitfalls and flaws, you can work on overcoming them to attain your goal. All this will make you more confident. Self-awareness is the basis for being able to take calculated risks in life.

LETTING GO OF THE PAST

When you hold onto any wrongdoings or mistakes made in your past, all that you do is hold onto unnecessary pain. When you cannot let go of the past, you will be unable to live in the present. Living in the present, the moment is what life is about. If you miss out on this, you will not be able to get anything done. With self-awareness comes acceptance. Once you accept your past, you can learn from your mistakes and then let it go. Let the past stay where it belongs- in the past! If you start being honest with yourself and are aware of all that's happening around you, it means that you aren't living in a fantasy world and are in the moment. You won't be living in a fantasy world in your head. Once you do this, then you can take the necessary steps to achieve your goals and make all the changes that are important to lead a happier life.

SETTING BOUNDARIES

Once you finally understand your potential and your limits, you can set healthy boundaries for yourself. Not just that, but you will be able to enforce them as well. By being self-aware of all this, you will not take up any such responsibilities that you know with certainty that you cannot fulfill. It doesn't mean that you will stop challenging yourself, but you will not accept any unnecessary stress.

Being self-aware means the ability to lead a life that's based on the knowledge of who you are and being brave enough to accept this and then share the same with the world. It isn't about being self-centered. It is about knowing yourself and your interactions with the world around you. Self-awareness teaches you to be kind to yourself and others. All this comes from understanding your self-worth and this needs introspection.

STEPS TO DEVELOP SELF-AWARENESS

Now that you are aware of what self-awareness is and the different benefits it offers, the next step is to learn to develop and increase self-awareness. You will learn about certain practical tips you can follow to meet this objective.

INTROSPECTION

The first thing that you must do is learn to see yourself clearly for who you are. This can be a rather tricky process, but with the right effort, you can get to know your real self and it will certainly be worth your while. When you can see yourself objectively, then you can start accepting yourself and work on ways to improve yourself.

The easiest way to get started with this process is to start by identifying your existing understanding of yourself and your perceptions about yourself. Take some time and make a note of all the things that you think you are good at doing along with the things that you must improve. Think about all those accomplishments that you are proud of or the things that you are proud of in your life. Think about your childhood and make a list of all the things that made you happy back then. What are the things that have changed and the ones that remained as is? What caused all these changes? If you aren't able to do this on your own, you can ask your loved ones to help you out initially. Start encouraging them to be honest with you regarding the way they feel about you and please don't take anything to heart. Take all the feedback that you receive in your stride. By the end of this exercise you will certainly have a fresh perspective of your life and your personality.

MAINTAIN A JOURNAL

Maintaining a journal is a great idea. You don't necessarily have to list your goals in it; you can simply use it to record your thoughts. This is a great way of reliving your mind of unnecessary thoughts and it helps clear some space up for new thoughts and ideas. Writing your thoughts in a journal is a way to declutter your mind. Ensure that you spend about 15-20 minutes per day writing your thoughts. It is best to do this activity before you go to sleep. Make a list of your feelings, the things you did well and the ones that you want to improve. This helps you move forward in life.

Think about all that you can do to help others, the things that you wished you can do-over and the things you want to improve about yourself. What do you value the most, what are your values and what is the most important task on your mind at present? When you pen down your thoughts, your mind will feel lighter. Also, it is a great way for self-reflection and helps you get a better idea of yourself.

RECORD YOUR GOALS AND PRIORITIES

It is quite similar to writing your thoughts in a journal. Plan your goals and make a list of them in the form of a worksheet. You can write down the step-by-step process to follow to attain your goals. Simplify a large goal into smaller ones so that it doesn't overwhelm you and you can start tackling them one by one.

SELF-REFLECTION

Self-reflection is essential for self-awareness. This means that you must set some time aside for this daily and honestly reflect upon yourself. Ensure that you make it a daily practice and stick to it. No one truly understands you the way you do and taking some time out of your schedule to reflect on your life is a good idea. You can start with about 15 minutes of self-reflection per day. Find a quiet spot for yourself and get started.

MEDITATION AND MINDFULNESS

Meditation is a great way to improve your self-awareness. There are different types of meditation you can use. You can use any of the easy breathing techniques to calm your mind.

The simplest way to meditate is to concentrate on your breathing. You must inhale and exhale, take deep long breaths. You can either sit or stand while doing this. You can open or close your eyes, whichever improves your focus. You can set aside a fixed time for this exercise, and this will help to make yourself used to do this every day. If you are trying to calm yourself down in a stressful situation, you can do this exercise. Take a deep breath through your nose for three seconds, and then hold onto your breath for two seconds and exhale for another 4 seconds. Repeat this for a few times, and you can calm yourself down.

While you are meditating, think about a couple of things like your goals, about whether the things you are doing will help you attain your goals or not, what are the obstacles you will face, what are the things you can improve and so on?

PERSONALITY TESTS

There are different psychometric and personality tests that you can take to determine your basic traits. They help increase your self-awareness. In such tests, there are no right or wrong answers. Instead, the questions you must answer will encourage you to dig deeper into your psyche and understand yourself better.

ASK OTHERS

By understanding what others think of you, you can learn more about yourself. You can ask your trusted friends and family members to honestly describe you. Ask them to be open and honest. Regardless of whether the feedback you receive is positive or negative, don't take it to heart. Instead, think of it as a means to understand yourself better. Make sure that you are only asking for feedback from those who have your best interest at heart and whom you fully trust. Also, if you feel like you need some clarity about anything that they bring up, don't hesitate while asking for the same. If you know that there is something about you that you want to change, then ask them to inform you about it the next time you engage in such behavior. For instance, if you have the habit of unconsciously interrupting others when they talk, then ask your friends to point this out the next time you do it so that you can rectify this behavior.

Apart from consulting your dear ones, you can also ask for feedback at work. When this is done well and is constructive, then such formal feedback can help you reflect upon your strengths and weaknesses with regard to your profession.

This process will take some while and to get to know yourself better, you need to be patient. The one thing that you must never do is give up or feel disheartened if you don't make any quick progress. Be patient with yourself!

CHAPTER FIVE: SELF-MANAGEMENT

The process of being able to manage yourself so that you can complete all the necessary tasks in a day to achieve success is referred to as self-management. Self-management is about learning to manage your time, planning your days and setting forth a plan of action to achieve your goals. Developing this skill is critical for growing in your life. If you don't, then you will never be able to unlock your true potential or work optimally.

INGREDIENTS OF SELF-MANAGEMENT

Self-management is quintessential for success. If you want to maximize your productivity and lead a happy and successful life, then you must work on developing the skill of self-management. All the great leaders are quite adept at self-management. In this section, you will learn about five self-management skills that you need to lead a happy and successful life- personal as well as professional.

POSITIVITY

There is no possible manner in which you can fake positivity. The genuine kind of positivity needs to come from within for it be visible on the outside. You must have a positive outlook towards life and your goals- both short and long-term ones. Constantly motivate yourself to achieve those goals with the help of positivity. As you start to achieve your goals you can witness a snowball effect. Focus on the end goal and keep doing at least one thing per day to ensure that you are a step closer to your goal. Acknowledge your success regardless of how small it is and don't be too hard on yourself. A brilliant thing about positivity is that it is infectious. Try to project your positivity on all those around you and you can build an environment that is positive at work as well as home.

SELF-AWARENESS

As I have mentioned in the previous chapter, being aware of your behavior along with the reasons for such behavior is an invaluable skill. You have probably come across people who are absolutely oblivious to their actions, their reasons and the effect that these actions have on others. Start to observe yourself objectively and learn to be your own manager. Initially, you might not like what your inner voice tells you. Don't become defensive and try to stay neutral. Self-awareness is a quintessential skill in life, but only a few know how to use it.

STRESS MANAGEMENT

Stress can ruin your life when it is left unchecked. If you are the sort that tends to make mountains out of molehills, then you stand the risk of burning yourself out. However, don't stress about it because there is an easy way out. Learning to manage stress comes handy given that we all lead extremely stressful lives these days. When you learn to manage stress, you can be pro-active in life instead of reacting in unfavorable and often negative manner.

Impulsive behavior like angry outbursts can drain your energy quickly. Instead of squandering away your precious energy on unnecessary things, learned to harness it to motivate yourself to do better in life. If a specific event makes you angry, instead of fueling that anger, use that event to motivate yourself.

The best way to manage stress is by waiting before you react and thinking of an effective solution for the situation. If you can delay your initial reaction, you can save yourself a lot of trouble. Take a couple of deep breaths and calm your mind before you make a decision. If you are facing an unpleasant situation, your initial reaction to it will also be negative. Instead of letting this negativity fester, you must try to calm your mind so that you can think logically before coming to any conclusions. For instance, if you have an argument with your spouse, harsh words are bound to be exchanged. Instead of indulging in this negative banter, take a moment to think about all the reasons for the argument and it will help you find an amicable solution. Only when your mind is calm can you react logically.

RESPONSIBILITY

Being aware of your actions and taking responsibility for them will bring you a step closer to self-management. From a young age we are all taught to assume responsibility for our actions. However, most of us don't do this. The first step is to prioritize all your responsibilities. Once you have your priorities in order, you can start tackling all those tasks that are important and then move on to the other things. Also, doing this helps you accept the responsibility for your actions. Never think of a mistake as failure, instead think of it is a chance to learn and do better. Slip ups are common and are bound to happen. Only when you accept your mistakes can you take the necessary corrective action. If you keep living in denial, then it is quite likely that you will keep repeating those mistakes.

PRODUCTIVITY

The best way to optimize your productivity is by effectively managing your downtime. If you have a huge pile of work that must be tackled, then ensure that you schedule sufficient breaks to prevent potential burnout. If you have some big event coming up, then ensure that you have the following weekend cleared out to recharge yourself. It is unlikely that you can work at 100% capacity always. After all, you are only human and accept this fact. Learning to manage your time and planning your day are important for self-management.

STEPS TO FOLLOW

In this section, you will learn about certain self-management tips that you can use at workplace as well as in your daily life.

LEARN ABOUT YOURSELF

Understanding yourself is the very first thing you need to do to fully understand your emotional intelligence. Once you get an idea of the extent of your emotional intelligence, you will realize how well you can express yourself. To understand how well you deal with your emotions, you must notice your behavior for a week and make notes about how you respond to different situations. Once you do this, you can start analyzing your behavior and actions so that you can notice all the different things that trigger an emotional reaction from you. Apart from this, you can also ask someone else to observe your behavior for a week and help you understand your emotions and the resultant actions. All this will help you gain a better understanding of yourself.

For instance, if you get to know that your Monday morning will be rather hectic, how will you react? If you feel irritated by the mere thought of all the work you have to do, then you must make a note of this negative reaction. Please understand that negative reactions can never generate favorable consequences. Make a list of all the things that upset you or trigger any negative feelings so that you can recognize them the next time they start to surface and stop them. It can be in the form of any personal conflicts. List down the things that upset you and your reaction to them. Note any clashes with leadership at work (reasons for the conflict and your reaction) and any stresses that elicited an overly emotional response from you and all the irritations at work that made you rather miserable.

You may not be aware of this now, but how you react to a stimulus affects how you work all day. Negative feelings will cause negative reactions, but how long can you stay cocooned in negativity? Can you let go of such situations or feelings? Do you harbor any negative feelings for someone at your workplace? Pay attention, because you do not know this now, but you will find that you are the cause of your misfortune because your reaction is what happens in your life. People with a low level of emotional intelligence will always blame others, not even realizing that their reaction is the factor that determines their degree of happiness, and not the actual trigger of emotions that they have experienced.

BECOME ADAPTABLE

Learning to adapt yourself is a great skill. You must adapt to your environment, regardless of what it is if you want to be successful in life. In general, someone likes a person who thinks like him. Therefore, you need to find a group of people in your workplace who share your beliefs, values or at least have similar opinions. If you are a part of a group where arguments and disagreements take place more often than not, then it simply proves that their levels of emotional intelligence are quite different from yours. So, try to find a group whose emotional intelligence matches yours. This not only helps you become better in the team, but also improves your productivity. However, if you cannot find such people or work with, then you must try to change in order to adapt to your environment. This means that you are ready to adapt, and people with high emotional intelligence can influence themselves without drastically altering their basic belief systems. They tolerate the actions of others and understand that it is only because they work with those who have low level of emotional intelligence. So, don't ruffle any feathers unnecessarily and learn to raise about it.

EMPATHY MATTERS

Empathy is a part of emotional intelligence. This is one of those elite qualities that can affect or break your emotional intelligence. When you perceive an emotion, you must not try to rebel against it. Instead, you must empathize and try to understand why a person can feel what he is doing. For instance, let us suppose that someone in the office is sad because she wasn't selected for a specific project. Then you must try to be empathetic towards that person and probably say something encouraging instead of saying something callous and blaming the person for it. Here, a person with high emotional intelligence can be distinguished from a person who has less. A person with a low level of emotional intelligence blames, while an emotionally intelligent person has empathy and is inclined to help others grow, rather than feel bad about their actions. They get better results through empathy and can teach their employees to respond better and get better results.

BECOME AN ACTIVE LISTENER

How do you feel when you are talking, and no one is paying any attention to you? You will feel bad and that's about it. The next reaction is that you will probably start resenting them for not listening to you. Now, imagine if others feel this about you? You don't want them to think that you are callous, do you? Being a good listener is an important life skill. To judge what other's feel and understand the emotions it elicits in you, you must pay attention. Only when you properly listen to others will you be able to formulate a well-thought-out response.

ANTICIPATE

To anticipate is simply to have an idea about a particular thing or situation. In this context, it means foreseeing what other people can say, and what emotions are behind it. It is useful to be prepared and prepared with a preconceived idea of what can be said, and you can develop a predetermined way of thinking. However, be sure to realize your thoughts only if they suit you. You can always create another emotion and create another thought if it is not. While waiting, you can communicate faster, better and more efficiently, saving time. It will help you if you want something from an employee or from your superior at work. If you have an idea of how your manager will respond, then you can use this to your advantage and come up with a question that will address his problems while conveying yours as well. For instance, if you want a person to be a part of your team even when your manager doesn't, then you can perhaps go about it in this manner:

"I know that you aren't too fond of her, but I want her to be involved in the team and I want to take full responsibility for her actions."

Thus, you recognized the negative feelings of your manager has towards the employee and made it clear that you are more than happy to help them solve the problem.

DIFFERENCES ARE COMMON

No two human beings are ever alike. I am not talking about physical attributes but about emotional and mental ones. This is applicable to all aspects of your life. There will be many people who think differently. Not everyone thinks alike, and it is impossible for everyone to think in the same manner. It is up to you whether you want to accept those differences or not. For instance, if something goes wrong at work, there will be some who immediately display their sadness and start thinking negatively, but then there will be some who think of the mistake as a learning opportunity and don't let it bother them too much. You must be able to relate to both types, and not just maintain a type that you think is right or one that feels the same as you.

You can use such differences to your advantage. Try to create a sense of understanding between people and try to group them according to the emotions that they display or the way they react. This helps with better communication while increasing participation from others.

LEARN TO DELEGATE

If you want to manage your work with emotional intelligence, you must be able to delegate work to your employees. Most leaders and successful people are adept at delegating work. Once a work has been delegated, then they transfer the problem to the other person and politely excuse themselves from that situation. For better productivity at work, you must learn to delegate. If you don't delegate, then you will merely overwhelm yourself with all the work that needs to be done. Before you start delegating, you must try to understand others and then give them work according to their capabilities to improve the overall productivity. You can communicate better with them because they are open to what you tell them. This seamless communication allows you to easily complete your daily business tasks and allows you to work easily and efficiently.

DELEGATE POWER

If you simply delegate your work, you will not get better results. In fact, you must delegate power when you delegate work and it helps to improve relationships. This gives people a sense of credibility and creates accountability so that they can make their own decisions and increase the efficiency of their work. But please observe caution while doing this. The person to whom you delegate work and power must have a good sense of emotional intelligence in order to take responsibility. If you end up delegating responsibility to someone who cannot measure up, you may have problems. Therefore, spend some time getting to know others before you start delegating.

BE RESPONSIBLE

There is a time when you have to take on a certain amount of guilt. You cannot constantly run away and must be able to control your feelings well enough. Many bosses will not take the blame, even if they are guilty or have done something that helps something go wrong. This only leads to problems in the workplace. To avoid them, you must improve your emotional intelligence. Humility and compassion are some of the qualities that will help you achieve this. Never be afraid to say that you did something wrong. It does not weaken you. In fact, it strengthens your position. People can communicate with others who understand their own boundaries and tend to respect them.

CHAPTER SIX: SOCIAL AWARENESS

Creating social connections is important for people, and emotional intelligence plays an important role in this institution. To increase your social presence, it is important to use your emotional intelligence. This will improve your overall development. This refers to how you interact with others and directly affects how they interact with you.

Although we looked at workplace situations in the previous chapter, this chapter is about how you can use your emotional intelligence in social situations. This will help you to express yourself as a person if you can use the information in this chapter to improve your relationship when you open up new opportunities.

COMMUNICATE EFFECTIVELY AND EFFICIENTLY

You cannot always think too much and worry too much about what you are going to say. It can negatively affect your emotional health. They must speak freely and without fear in order to win friends and allies.

If you keep rethinking things before you say them, you will not be able to communicate anything. Communication is very important in a relationship, so you must be able to freely communicate your feelings without fear that they will be judged. Remember that you will not be judged for what you say when you speak with confidence. However, unsafe behavior causes others to doubt you and puts your credibility at risk. Trust is important in friendship, so speak as freely as possible.

They say it's great for your relationship. Remember, however, that in your comments you become less frivolous when you change your thinking and try to make your social circle more compassionate. Check yourself and write down things that caused a bad reaction. Then look at what happened in these circumstances so that you can find the best approach to this issue in the future. You need to remember that no matter how honest you are in communicating with other people, sometimes you say the wrong things at the wrong time not because you are less honest, but because you speak with not as sensitive as you will like. They cannot dictate what other people feel. However, as soon as you discover that they feel bad or have problems, you can use your emotional intelligence to help them get out of trouble and feel good again.

People who are open, honest and can speak freely will also pick up the moods of others and will be able to adapt the conversation to the situation. People without emotional intelligence do not distinguish and often blame others for inconsistency. You must be assertive, but not enough to ridicule or humiliate others. Once you have dealt with your bad situation, you are also the first to try to help them, and therefore you like people like you. They do not give you advice that makes you feel that you are overloading someone with your feelings. Emotionally intelligent people can adapt their conversation to those things that others may not even notice.

ACTIVE LISTENING

I cannot stress the importance of active listening. It is so important that you listen carefully to others. There must be a balance between what you say and what you listen to, and you cannot always expect people to listen to you, and you are not listening. If you do not listen to others, they are not interested in what you say. How often do you notice that people ask what you are doing and then leave before you get an answer? This is a common occurrence and shows a complete lack of sympathy for another person. Although it may be politically correct to ask people who they are, emotionally intelligent people are actually waiting for the answer of the questioner because they have enough attention to listen.

Hearing is also necessary because your thoughts and emotions are controlled. If you do not listen to others, you develop irrational thoughts or emotions, and reacting to them causes problems. Listening to others helps establish simple communication between people. It also makes you a good friend. If there are people in your social environment who are dissatisfied, you will hear prompts to understand that most of their dissatisfaction is related to their reaction to certain stimuli. You have to say that not everyone sees things as much as the person who insulted them, but they must be thick-skinned when other people can invade their heads.

FOSTER UNDERSTANDING

Empathy and understanding are a big part of social intelligence, and you have to be good at both in order to be good in a group. Friendship can continue only when emotional intelligence is involved. If this is not the case, the two people involved cannot communicate very effectively, and this misunderstanding causes problems. Therefore, people with low emotional intelligence are encouraged to work on improving their emotional intelligence. The next time you talk to a friend, try to regain your mood. Try to listen to what they are saying and try to understand their situation before looking for solutions. This means practicing empathy, and empathy is something that people with great emotional intelligence are very good at.

When you listen to a conversation and see who controls the conversation, people usually think about themselves more than they do about their audience. These are those holes in life that offer little sympathy and do not really listen and do not try to understand others because they consider themselves independent. In fact, they are tactless and probably have big problems in their own lives. You may not know that you are not listening to people, and you will surely be shocked if you offer it. Learn from watching because you immediately recognize people with a low level of emotional intelligence.

One thing you will notice is people who have adapted to their high level of emotional intelligence, because they are people who stand out from the crowd, and everyone wants to be a friend.

MAKING NEW FRIENDS

To succeed, you need a reasonable network of people. To build this network, you need to make good use of your social intelligence. Thus, you can attract new, especially powerful people and make new friends in your social circle. This is very important if you want to make progress in life. Having better connections increases your chances for a better job and makes it interesting for you.

When you make new friends, do not forget to use your emotional intelligence to maintain good relationships. It does not mean being so clever - or even smarter - than a new friend. This is not a matter of sole prowess. It means being yourself and being aware that it is worth getting to know a new friend. You do not have to impress. You must listen, learn, and use your emotional intelligence to know when to listen and when to speak. In general, those with a high emotional intelligence will immediately recognize this. However, if you still do not know your emotional intelligence, take every conversation as it is, and never be jealous when someone else is in the center of attention. Your emotional intelligence means that you have the good sense to know that there are no real stars. There are only people, and the more a new girl communicates, the more opportunities to learn about him, and this is very good.

MAINTAINING RELATIONSHIPS

People often say that friendship is not constant and that over time everything must disappear. This is not at all true, and you must not consider this as practical advice. Maintaining relationships is always beneficial for you, and it is very possible to use your emotional intelligence and realize that a certain degree of mutual concessions is required to maintain relationships. Yes, the dynamics of relationships will change over time, and your emotions will change. However, you can adapt to new situations until you give up and leave irrational thoughts in your head.

For instance, if a friend of yours shifts to another city, then you must be open-minded enough to know that you feel not only an absence, but also yourself. Additional call to your friend when he is in a new setting is always welcome. Staying in touch means keeping them in your social circle, even when you are far away from each other. With social networks, Skype calls and e-mail, there is no reason to deprive them of their lives just because they live in another city. When you stay in touch, you have a lot of emotional intelligence, since you make yourself available to a wider audience of friends, and your relationship stays longer.

CHAPTER SEVEN: RELATIONSHIP MANAGEMENT

Did you ever feel overwhelmed by all your emotions and then ended up saying certain things that you regretted the moment you uttered them? Well, all this keeps happening more often than anyone cares to admit. Who doesn't slip up every now and then when their emotions overwhelm them and end up messing up something good, they have in their lives?

The truth is that it will probably be useful for all of us to learn how to control and manage our emotions in a more constructive way. Can you imagine all the unnecessary clashes, struggles and tears that you could have and still can save yourself from if you probably controlled your emotions better? Emotional intelligence is considered to be one of the most important aspects of modern psychology, and for good reason. Emotional intelligence is associated not only with great satisfaction in relationships, but also with improving your work and improving your stress management skills. It is about making sure that you control your emotions and not vice versa. If you really want to build deeper and more meaningful relationships with your friends, colleagues, or even your partner, a relationship that goes beyond superficial conversations will be very useful if you put the development of emotional intelligence as one of your top priorities in your to-do list. But what is emotional intelligence and how to improve it?

Simply put, emotional intelligence is the ability to recognize and regulate the emotions that you experience, empathizing with others and aware of their reaction. It is about balancing the awareness of your emotions and the emotions of others. At the same time, emotional intelligence helps you effectively manage your relationships, even when conflicts or differences arise. Well, the good news is that emotional intelligence can be developed through exercise. The tips in this section will help you strengthen your relationship by developing emotional intelligence.

The importance of self-awareness cannot be stressed enough. The cornerstone of emotional intelligence is self-awareness, which means that you must understand yourself before trying to understand others. If you know yourself well enough, you can better understand how you can meet other people. To increase your self-esteem, you need to focus on your strengths, triggers, values, morality, etc., so that you can see things that positively affect you. If you know about such things, the next time you feel that you have an emotional outburst; you can make a conscious effort not to go this way.

You must be open not only for feedback, but also for criticism. It is very likely that not everyone agrees on what you say or do, but it will be very helpful if you can evaluate the opinions of others before making a decision. Instead of getting rid of blind spots, you can use the feedback you received to determine your behavior, which negatively affects your life. They must be able to constructively accept criticism, and not to consider it as humiliation, but as an opportunity to learn something new.

If you want to develop your emotional intelligence, it is helpful to have a diary in which you can record events, your feelings, emotions, and how you responded to them. Your reaction can be physical, emotional, or even physiological. You can create a list of your roles and feelings that you will associate with these roles. Think of the different roles you play in your life, the roles of your wife, husband, mother, father, sister, brother, employee, employer, and so on. Think of as many roles as possible and of the various feelings that you will associate with these roles. Then you can predict what you will feel. You can do this by thinking about the situation you are in, and then predict how you will feel in such a situation. You must practice the challenge and even accept the feeling that you feel frustrated, angry, or helpless. When you evoke these feelings, you gain some control over these feelings. As soon as you control your feelings, you can respond accordingly. It helps you to perceive your emotional triggers.

You must make a conscious effort to be attentive in all areas of your life. This means that you must start looking attentively at others and stop judging them. By learning to observe both your thoughts and your emotions, you can raise your awareness of perceptions, and instead of making assumptions; you can gain clarity to think things through. When you look after yourself, the likelihood of negative emotions overtaking your body decreases significantly.

We all tend to experience emotions physically. Therefore, when we are emotionally stressed, our body tends to react physically. This leads to an increase in blood pressure, cholesterol, and so on. None of this is desirable from afar. If you can soothe how your body reacts to stress, you can successfully deal with the emotional component of the body. You must take steps to eliminate stress in the bud. If you feel tense, just breathe deeply. You need to focus on slow breathing and slow breathing. This will help you to remove the stress ball that accumulates inside you. In this case, you can better cope with the emotional situation.

Never forget that there are several ways to see the same incident. Instead of giving up on negative emotions when you get upset about someone else's actions, it will be better to calm down a bit and take the time to approach the story from the perspective of another to analyze. What seems deliberate to you can only be a genuine mistake. Let your anger pass before you decide to do something rash, think calmly and calmly. Ask the stories that you think have happened, even if you think they are true. Looking at an incident from a neutral perspective can definitely change your

Jacob Fitzgerald

point of view.

CHAPTER EIGHT: TIPS FOR BETTER EMOTIONAL INTELLIGENCE

DEAL WITH NEGATIVE EMOTIONS

The most important aspect of emotional intelligence is probably your ability to cope with your negative emotions. Controlling emotions, so that they do not overwhelm you and do not cloud your judgment, is really important to you. To change how you feel in a situation, you need to change your thinking. Here are a couple of instances that will help you understand this point.

NEGATIVE PERSONALIZATION

It is typical for us to feel unfavorable towards someone and his behavior. This may lead us to conclusions, but it is important that we do not do this. Instead, we must try to look at the situation differently. Try to find different angles before you respond. Take the instance of a friend who did not answer your call. You may be tempted to believe that she is ignoring you, but think about it. There is no reason why your friend starts to ignore you for no reason. She may be busy right now. You will take this into account only if you avoid personalizing the behavior of people. Everyone does his job more than he thinks about how his behavior affects other people. Therefore, it is important that you expand your point of view and avoid misunderstandings. You do not know what is happening with this absent friend and assume that you have no mind at all. The best way forward will be to break the ice at the first opportunity when he called this friend. You may find that you have extended a friendship and that your friend might have thought that you have lost interest in her.

FEAR OF REJECTION

You must always give yourself more opportunities in an important situation. This ensures that you have reliable alternatives if the action plan fails. This is a truly effective way to overcome the fear of failure. Never put all your eggs in the basket. I am sure that you have heard this expression, but if you are so addicted to a person that you suffer from disappointment, if you are disappointed, you are subject to injury. Now you can apply this to your emotions. Think of Plan B and even Plan C as you approach the situation. Do not assume the worst if your date does not appear. Just do something yourself and wait for their explanations. In fact, it may be something completely innocent that prevented this person from appearing, but you will never know if you blame him for leaving you. Learn to be smart and not in need of others. Yes, it was not foolish not to show up, but things happen that are out of people's control, and sometimes you have to admit that plans change as well.

COPING WITH STRESS

A certain amount of stress is commonplace for most of us. What sets us apart is stress management. When you do well with stress, everything can be the difference between reactivity and assertiveness, between estrangement and satiety. Always keep cooling when you are under pressure. Here are two simple tips you can follow.

Whenever you are either nervous or angry, wash your face with cold water and go out for some fresh air. By cooling the temperature around you, you reduce your fear. Also, remember to avoid caffeine. It stimulates nervousness. Another way to cope with this is to simply go out into the fresh air and breathe slowly and purposefully, as this helps to balance the oxygen in your body. When people experience stress, they are prone to hyperventilation. If you know each other well and know what you are doing, then fresh air and calm breathing will help you return to your perspective.

If you are depressed, frustrated or anxious, then head to the gym for intense aerobic exercise. This will revitalize your body and mind and make you feel much better. Movement determines emotions, as they say. Whenever you want to feel more secure, exercise and experience the vitality of your body. It will make you blossom with adrenaline, and this may be all you need to actually cope with the situation in such a way as to strengthen you, rather than throwing energy.

LEARN TO EXPRESS DIFFICULT EMOTIONS

We often face situations in our lives where we have to set our limits so that people know where we are. There are many situations where it is important for you to remain assertive and express your point of view. They have the right to contradict, without offending, reject the request, not feeling guilty, setting their own priorities and protecting themselves from coercion or harm. This is all an integral part of an adult. You must recognize these times when you need to make the right decisions.

When dealing with difficult emotions, it's easy to be overwhelmed. But there is one method that suits me, if I want to express difficult feelings, the XYZ technique. This can be explained with a simple sentence: I feel X if you do Z Y in a situation.

DEALING WITH DIFFICULT PEOPLE

There are a lot of unreasonable people, and you will ever meet. Perhaps you are stuck with someone like this at work or even at home, and it's easy for such people to spoil our day if we let them. To cope with such difficult people, you need to take the initiative. Here are a couple of things that you can do.

Take a deep breath and slowly count to ten if you feel angry or upset about someone. This ensures that you don't say anything you might regret later. In nine out of ten cases, you will calm down and find a way to better cope with the situation when you've finished counting. This reduces the problem, not aggravates it. If you are still upset about the problem, take a break and visit it later when you calm down. When you approach the topic, when you feel crazy, do not use your emotional intelligence.

You do not want to be reactive; you want to be active. So, try for a moment to put yourself in the position of another person. It is difficult, but it gives you a perspective. Think about the other person and his situation, and then tell yourself how difficult it is to be in this situation.

COPING WITH ADVERSITIES

Did you know that Michael Jordan missed more than 9,000 shots in his career and lost nearly 300 games? He missed the victory shots when he was trusted to make these shots. But the great thing is that he got up every time he failed or was crushed. That's the reason for his success.

It is important to know that you do not always get what you want, and that life is sometimes hard. Life often challenges us, and how we deal with it matters. You may hope or despair, you may be optimistic or disappointed, but it will affect everything when you approach the situation. Think half of this mug if you have a situation where you need to make a decision or move. Think about the overall situation. Look at it from your point of view, as well as from another person. This gives you much more control than you can have if you only saw your side of the coin.

Regardless of how the situation develops, you must ask yourself if you have learned something from this experience and what is the future ahead of what is more important now. Ask yourself good questions and get quality answers that will help you prioritize and learn to live a full life. You get perspective and cope much better with future situations.

EXPRESSING INTIMACY

In any intimate relationship, it is important to show love and affection. Your ability to effectively express and test these emotions plays an important role in the development of your personal relationships. "Effective" here means that you share your feelings with another person in a constructive, nourishing and positive way and show them that you are well aware of their feelings and fertilize each other. Never be afraid to break your barriers when it comes to intimate relationships. People who are free in their emotional relationship and can show appreciation and love will always have a better relationship than those who hold back.

Any method of positive communication, through which people express intimate emotions in relationships, according to Dr. John Gottman called the "commandment." Positive eye contact and gestures such as smiling, hugging, hugging the shoulders, can be considered as a requirement of body language. Telling others how you feel about them is oral bidding. There is another kind of commandment, behavioral laws. Doing something that adds value to someone's life like giving them a thoughtful gift helps develop intimacy and is a part of a behavioral offer.

CONCLUSION

I want to thank you once again for purchasing this book. I hope it proved to be an enjoyable and an informative read.

Emotional intelligence plays an important role in all aspects of your life. So, learning to improve your emotional intelligence is the key to leading a happier and a more successful life.

Now, all that you need to do is get started by implementing the simple steps given in this book to improve your emotional intelligence. Learning to control and manage your emotions isn't a skill that you can learn overnight. It will take some time and constant practice. So, please don't give up and do keep trying. Every day you follow these steps, you will be a step closer to success in life.

Thank you and all the best!